Like Salted Caramel

M.J. Valencia Esparza

For you; who made me *cry, love, learn* and *live*.
I have never felt as alive as when I was next to you.
Thanks for everything. My heart will forever be yours.

A tí, a quien tanto amo.
Porque nada es para siempre, pero tú y yo, somos infinito.

Contents:

ache
realization
withdrawal
soothe

"The enormous appeal of this sweet and salty combination is simple, seeing as blending two flavors doubles the taste sensation. Moreover, people generally like sweet because it brings pleasure and comfort, while salt is enjoyable (at the right ratio) due to its flavor-enhancing abilities. Furthermore, the mineral is essential to the healthy function of our bodies. Keep in mind, while too much salt can taste terrible, a subtle sprinkle over a sweet base will stimulate the taste buds and create a pleasurable experience."

Camille Hawkey 2016, The Long-Lasting Craze of Salted Caramel
P Magazine Issue 7

Our love tastes like salted caramel.

ache

And they grew tired,

           of talking,
           of speaking,
           of laughing,
           of hugging,
           of touching,
           of feeling,

                              of being…

No one told me the membership for love,
expires after 7 years.

No renewable
options.

I love you.

So very deep, my nails could feel it,

my lashes could feel it,

my freckles could feel it.

Can you still feel it too?

M.J. Valencia Esparza

The smell of love might not be sweet after all…

Like Salted Caramel

Is it too late for us?
To kiss our lips and touch our souls.
To hug our bodies and fill our lungs with that honeyed smell.

To see your eyes, and go on without all this despair.

Love hurts when you are meant to love for a lifetime, in the short span of seven years.

I'm trying to fit a plum tree into a flower vase

Like Salted Caramel

My need for you is devastating:

Your eyes.
Your laugh.
Your lips.
Your smell.
Your kiss.
Your soul.

You are my type of cancer.
You have spread all over my body.
Now it is too late, for I know it is the terminal type.

I´m in love with three people at once:

- the first one hurts
- the second one neglects
- the third one loves

You are the first two, but when there is a full moon, number three is visible too.

Three is an odd number

My safe haven has been torn apart.
There is no home to go to.
Perhaps, I have escaped from it,
from you.

I am a runaway.

Why

    break

        someone

            to

                mend

                    her

                        again?

Ways to practice masochism inversely

Our love poem:

Me, Amsterdam.
Me and you Barcelona.
You and me, Paris.
Us, Forever.

Lies can come in various shapes: in texts, in calls, in words, in promises…

                                        In the shape of you.

A horror story is not that of ghosts, demons, monsters…
A horror story is made up of real life situations.

Me needing you and you not needing me in the same way is a
perfect example.

Don't let anyone treat you like an asteroid
when you are a fucking constellation.

We don't speak **love** in the same language.

                                            And communication **is key.**

In the end… I always end up hitting the same wall; making me reach the same conclusion…

I love you, with no doubts, with no regrets, with no control.

M.J. Valencia Esparza

Love is ~~blind~~.
~~I am~~ bullshit.

Foolish to say you are my everything,
when everything reduces to nothing,
without you.

Perhaps my attention was not enough, so you carried on
looking for pretty eyes to see and hear the
pretty words you had to say…

But love is not pretty with three pairs of ears.

The sole presence of you was enough for me: your skin, your chin, your laugh, your smell, your eyes… and my presence came unnoticed to you.

Tachycardia.

        When you look at me.
        When you speak to me.
        When you touch me.
        When you kiss me.
        When you make love to me.

                When you say "I love you."
                When you decided to leave.

I crave you, I scream for you, I ache because of you.
I beg you for something, you are not capable of giving.

When you spend half of your life with someone, you slowly start becoming that person and vice-versa.

When you leave that person for good, you feel lost and empty and vice-versa.

When will you finally be certain of me,
for I am tired of waiting. You are not into me enough
to run away together and leave everything behind.

You, me, us, together.

        Not today.

                Not after 7 years.

                        Not ever.

You bastard, how dare you make love to me for almost a decade, caress my body, play with my hair, rub my cheeks and fill me up with sweet, sweet love.

You bastard, you asshole, you idiot, you prick, you, You, YOu, YOU.

YOU.

I love you so much, yet, I am not sure about you.

Why are you so certain about me….

 Am I the bad guy?

Have you lied to me?!?!
I. Should. Not.
Be needing to ask this question.
And yet, here I am.
For the 20th time.

Life without you is a canvas with splashes of color:
bright, pale, dull and they all mix together.

Now, describe me, your canvas.

You are selfish.
You are careless.
You are not mine anymore.

In the end we don't belong together.

I miss you so much, it turns my insides.

VOMITING ~~LOVE~~
                LONELINESS

Fall in love
Fight
Cry
Make Out
Fall in love
Fight again
Make love
Kiss
Cry
Fight…

                                                The chronicles of Us

Your love is too genuine, too much, too perfect….

This can't last forever.

This can't be real.

This can't be true.

This can't be love.

And yet here you are… after 7 years, with a love and a kind heart that can't be mine forever. Can't continue on growing beautifully after all our flaws, my flaws….

Like Salted Caramel

Fairytales do exist.
Shut the outer noise, you won't notice it otherwise.

You feel like home.

A place to rest, to sleep, to love.

That night you told me, you didn't know who you were anymore, what you wanted, who you loved…

I was pretty sure I loved you far beyond comprehension… and just then, it started to sunrise.

If I were to be a cassette, you would be the hand clicking on the fast forward button.

I will leave as soon as I recover my strength, re-arm my broken heart, regain what you've taken without even knowing. For I am not gonna be that girl, the one "living her life hoping you realize you can't live yours without me in it."

What Kaur taught me.

You displayed a total lack of character when it actually mattered.

Timing is everything.

I have come to the realization…

The greater the distance that's keeping us apart, the greater the love I feel for you.

Perhaps the problem was me being hard to earn, not to get.

Humans are not perfect; we however, keep obsessing and playing with the concept.

We forget we are human and that is why we are in love.

If perfection does not exist, I don't know how we remain together, passionate, happy and devoted to each other.

I find myself constantly thinking how much
I would *love you to love me* in the same way I do. However,
that is egocentric, that is not love, that is needy and most
importantly, that is impossible.

I don't know if you are the love of my life, for the flaws we've made makes **US** feel like a huge mistake. All **I** want is to keep on doing **YOU**.

The love you give to me, is not the kind of love
I would give myself.

Resting souls in numbers

4 a.m. in the morning,
2 humans lying in the same bed,
10 cm apart from each other,
26 degrees °C and still, he pulls her into his arms.

What is love?

It became a struggle to remind you how much you loved me…
When love is not meant to be reminded, it is meant to be felt.

Today I'm empty.
I feel no sadness,
or anger,
or happiness.

I feel no fear,
or love.

I feel nothing; for all I had I gave it away.

			You have left me soulless.

I come from Venus and you are an astronaut who has landed
on the wrong planet.

Like Salted Caramel

I loved you profoundly and still chose to move countries away. Now that we are no longer in the same time zone I start to realize, we were never even in the same orbit.

Reality check:

You are no longer here,
you are no longer mine.

There are various ways in which love can be expressed:

- Soft and tender kisses between the thighs.
- Holding hands on the street and not letting go once you arrive at your destination.
- Spontaneous kisses on the lips or cheeks.
- A discrete squeeze of the but when in public.
- Delicate kisses on the forehead.
- Hugs that can literally take your breath away.
- Texts saying "Hello, I love you."

We grew apart together.

I am insane and you were never the cure,
but the reason for my illness.

You knew it was coming, yet you were careless
of the apocalypse…

A crashing meteorite in Paris.

Only fools fall in love.

You think I'm a fool.

You fell in love with me.

Love is foolish, we are not.

We are real.

Reminder: ugly souls can come in pretty packages.

I *hate* you
I *love* you
I *am* sorry
I *am* lonely
I *love* you
I *love* me

I *leave* you.

Why are you so full of yourself, didn't your mamma tell you "happiness is only real when shared?"

                                              Lessons in life

I had to be surrounded by complete silence, in order to start listening to his heartbeat.

Then I remembered, deaf hearts feel nothing.

I want someone who can put me first.
Not for duty or with effort,
but for love.

Like Salted Caramel

You said 'I adore you' and then turned me into a goddess. Your worshiping lasted 48 months, until you decided to become an atheist.

I think I got lost trying to help you find out who you were and what you wanted, when all along, I always knew myself in that matter.

If text messages were enough to show interest, phones would not have a "call" button.

Technology is meant for the lazy lovers

I have only experienced sex with love
   … it fucked me pretty bad.

Things don't end.
They transform after being hurt so much.

Learn to be grateful.

I took you and many other things for granted.

If we belong together why do we keep drifting apart?

What movies don't teach you about love.

It is always always in the details, time and empathy.

I am your Juliet.

Fuck my Romeo.

For every mile that is keeping us apart, a tear that rolls down my cheek. For every day we spend far away from each other, a heartbeat less from mine pumping for yours.

Don't you know that leaving a heart that is so in love… only brings serious consequences?

I will not waste 7 more years, waiting for you to choose me when all this time I have been choosing you.

Now, I AM CHOOSING MYSELF.

Some people don't deserve the love they were given.
Like humans don't deserve Mother Earth and nature.

Evolving from your heartbreak

From: ME
To: ME

Not in a million years will you be able to stand to the height the woman next to you is standing. Not if you fail to recognize the miracle you have got by your side.

Women are walking miracles

Wrong percentage %

How much of my insecurities is really reflected on you not missing me and how much is it me wanting you to do so?

withdrawal

Like Salted Caramel

Fell in love so hard, that when I did hit the ground
in dust I converted.

There are plenty of fish in the sea, but we are not fish, we are humans and some of us can't swim at all.

My favorite type of holes are resting on a pair of cheeks, coming alive whenever a smile is formed for the world to see them.

Give me 2,739 roses, one per day we've been together.

Give me chocolates, give me kisses, give me a ring, give me love, give me life.

Give me us for now…forever.

Seven months later, 9,216 km apart,
4 beers and 2 glasses of wine taken tonight and still can't learn that you can run away from people, but not from feelings.

I have been a fool for so many years. I see this way of living as my only reality.

Wake up girl, dreams are not meant to last forever.

To love in the way you love me could be seen as an adjective, not a verb.

Therefore I am about to scream: take action!

For all I know is I love you.
Through the good, the bad, the fights, the laughs,
the distance...

In my perfect world,
I am the first thing you see in the morning,
the last before you go to bed and the only
one when you start dreaming.

Do you think of me when I am away?

Silly questions from a stupid girl…

Be sweet…

                        Be mine…

                                                  Be here…

                        Be present…

                      Be in love with me again.

Story of a coward who:

Moved seas away from the one she loved, yet 9,210 km were not enough for her to stop loving him.

Cigarette

I.

Stop killing yourself. It is killing me to see you do it.

II.

His favorite thing against his lips was never my own.

His hands caressing my face was a poem on its own.
The music made by our lips was a song in C mayor.

If you are "the one for me" like you have said on so many occasions…

Why have I shed so many tears for the one "meant to be"?

The lies you keep

She left
She was gone
She disappeared

From you
From your life
From your sight
From your heart

I love you. The real you, the one that does not fake it, or forces it or matches perfectly within this society and this world. I love you. The one who kisses me gently on the forehead for no reason, the one who laughs at stupid jokes and smiles when his eyes meet mine.
I love you, E.

You and me were made forever,
in a world in which everything is only temporary.

Why would you give up on me, on us, on you?

- I demand a reason for your behavior -

Deep down we both know…
You'll never be able to stop loving, feeling, craving or missing ME.

Like Salted Caramel

You belong to me as much as I belong to you. It is not about property, but about who the heart chooses to blend with.

TO DO LIST:

1. you
2. you
3. you
4. you
5. you get the idea

If I close my eyes and focus, I can recreate the feeling of your hand playing with my hair, the smell of your perfume which became stronger as my face rested against your chest. You are the scent of love flooding my lungs.

If I focus enough, I can feel you with my heart and smell you with my memories.

A three letter poem:

Y O U

Like Salted Caramel

Insanity was given to me in the shape of a 1.88 meter, olive skin male with big dark eyes, kind smile and full lips.

Come crash my dreams, my heart and my bed again.
I miss you.

Reckless 3am thoughts

Everything… ends

Very   Violently

When it comes to passionate love.

You are my worst habit, good thing one can train to make these go away.

Soon you'll be gone from my life.
~~heart~~
~~mind~~
~~soul~~

I am pretty sure we have met in our past lives...
Now I wonder how many more will have to pass for us to finally end up together...

Our happy ending is yet to come.

The laughing, the dancing nights that went on and on like your kisses, your hugs, the good times…

… (at some point) we were the best love story.

Like Salted Caramel

The City of love took mine.
Paris broke my heart.

Why do we choose to be far away from the one we love?

The days go by and you are not here. I can tell you don't care. For you saying I love you on the phone is just as valid as when it comes from your lips with my face upfront.

The way you treat us is not important, therefore you are not important to me either.

Stay there, in the City of love, for the one I had to offer was not enough to keep you by my side and so, I came to the conclusion:
Giving up is not for cowards, but for wise people.

You were always good at hiding things from me.

For example:
At hiding that you miss me, you are the fucking champion.

soothe

Thank you for being a smiling person.

Our love wasn't good, great, bad or terrible.
Our love was human and that made us fools (for each other).

You are your greatest discovery, your greatest war and your greatest love.

Learn to see this and you'll be able to fall in love for the first time; during the second time, you'll fall for another person.

He was not everything.
Everything is just the tiny bits summed up and he was just a part of them.

A kind smile, a warm hand, a coke with a burger, a stupid fight and an immeasurable kind of love.

His memory will remain, like a ketchup stain on my heart.
(sticky, sweet and hard to get off)

I crave for so much more than what I was given, and that is not greed, it is me accepting I deserve a love story. I will give it to myself, the greatest of them all, surrounded by passion, emotion and power.

I kept reaching out for you. I had grown very used to silence, to indifference, to hostility.

> No need for that word trio anymore.

I loved you.
(applies for present and future tense as well)

What we are as humans:

If we stop to think about it…
We are, but an instant that has been prolonged,
making us believe in the possibility of one day becoming infinite.

The love you have for you, the love you give yourself, is the love you show others to give you.
Period.

Make your conclusions:

You haven't shed a tear in a year.
Either for joy, happiness, sorrow, fear or love.

Tears are filled with feelings and in the absence of them....

Oh how marvelous it will be, the day you come to love someone as much as you love yourself.

Letter to the love of my life:

I am sorry I tried to find you in someone else when you were right here all along.

From: Me
To: Myself

I took my hand and placed it on the left side of my temple. I got quiet for a bit and stayed really still… After months of silence, I heard it again.

My heart is beating and my heartbeat is a song.

Darling,
Stop judging yourself; when you know you are worth so much more than what you were given.

Live, learn, grow.

Block his number, enjoy summer, get a tan, swim,
eat ice-cream, meet people, go away, look for adventure,
know different countries, learn to love yourself with passion.

(instructions on how to forget your ex)

The lies you told me,
I kept them in a box for years.
It was like keeping trash in a basement,
useless and only taking up space.
So I took them out.
Basement is empty.

Go, grow, learn, have fun, enjoy, experience, become a better person, a better human and in the process, we can both learn to be alone together.

Love deeply, with no fear… once you reach a certain depth, you'll bump into "self - love."

Only then will you know that it is time to resurface.

Our eyes have seen how beautifully we have grown together.
Imagine what we could end up being
if we keep on growing up like this.

Find someone that makes you bloom in pretty colors,
do the same for them during this process…

At the end you will have a flower garden.

Took me some time,
some pain,
some tears,
some laughs,
some years,
To find the love of my life...

Myself.

I want you to want me as much as I fantasize about it.
But mom taught me avarice is a terrible thing and
you are not necessarily made in gold material.

One day I will stop writing about you and
I cannot help but wonder:
Who will I write about next?

I still think about you out of time and space.

You are my fifth dimension.

Never have I grown so much internally, as the times we grew apart from each other.

By now, several times I have wondered…
Is this the beginning of our end?

Since you left, I have been feeling a hole in my body which I have slowly been filling up with self love.

Of two things I can be certain:

1. You love me unconditionally.
2. You are not here anymore.

The universe is us.
It is everything and it is nothing.

When love is real and genuine, there will never be an ending to it.

For love will continue to expand, re-shape and become the best version of itself.

You choosing to leave me, is making me choose to leave you.

Distance is not meant for lovers.

I am so much more.
I can give so much more,
than what you are willing to in our relationship.

Hope you are getting used to croissants and espresso.

                              I will never have them for breakfast again.

The more I think about it,
the more certain I am of our ending.

> Your heart is made of stone and mine
> is made of flowers.

>> Sometimes, a flower grows in between
>> the cracks of pavement, but it is never
>> the other way around.

At night it hurts the most.
The memories kick hard and fast against my chest.
The tears roll down my cheeks in the same manner.
As I lay in bed, holding on to my pillow, I realize soon it will be morning.

Through the cracks of my curtains I start to see sunlight.
Then I stop crying.

Everything that comes from the heart is done with love.

Everything done with love is well done.

Like Salted Caramel
First Edition

Copyright © M.J. Valencia Esparza 2020

All Rights Reserved
No part of this publication may be reproduced
without written permission from the author.

ISBN: 978-1-8381678-4-4

www.ingramcontent.com/pod-product-compliance
Lightning Source LLC
Chambersburg PA
CBHW021438080526
44588CB00009B/579